Still Prospering

Autumn Smith

WESTBOW
PRESS®
A DIVISION OF THOMAS NELSON
& ZONDERVAN

WestBow Press books may be ordered through booksellers or by contacting:

WestBow Press
A Division of Thomas Nelson & Zondervan
1663 Liberty Drive
Bloomington, IN 47403
www.westbowpress.com
844-714-3454

ISBN: 978-1-6642-5946-1 (sc)
ISBN: 978-1-6642-5947-8 (hc)
ISBN: 978-1-6642-5945-4 (e)

Library of Congress Control Number: 2022903887

Print information available on the last page.

WestBow Press rev. date: 3/29/2022

Dedication

To Devin Mathes, my big brother and first best friend: you have truly made my world so much better. Thank you for all the deep political and theological conversations during quarantine. I love you.

To Tanna Mathes: thank you for loving my brother and raising my beautiful niece. You make our family a million times happier. I love you.

To Emmy Mathes: I will never know how my brother made something as beautiful as you. Please never lose your creativity and enthusiasm. I love you.

Kyiwann Smith: you are the most brilliant and handsome young man in the entire world. Thank you for letting me be your "bonus" mom regardless of circumstance. I love you forever.

Contents

Foreword

Two hours. My copy of Autumn's first book, *Prospering*, was clenched in my hands for two hours before I could bring myself to open its pages. I stared at the stunning photo of my sister (by choice—who needs pesky birth records?), my cheerleader, my fierce defender, devoted prayer partner, and my genuine friend. Proud and excited, I finally opened Autumn Smith's book prepared to marvel at how I would be touched. Would I laugh, cry, gain wisdom? Yes. All of it. What I didn't expect, however, was the familiarity. Even her penned words carry innate authenticity and made me feel exactly as I do in her presence: full of light and joy, always heard, always seen. That is a gift.

John C. Maxwell once wrote, "The thing I love about writing books is it allows me to talk to many people I will never personally meet." It's the spirit behind that statement that gives me deep gratitude that Autumn choses to write. There are many people she will never meet personally. If not for this medium, many people might miss the opportunity to experience her unique ability to make every soul she encounters feel its worth.

Encounters with others generally leave a fingerprint, usually on our soul. Some leave a fingerprint that will expose your weakness. Conversely, Autumn leaves a fingerprint that effortlessly floods a light on all that is beautiful within you.

This is exquisitely apparent in one of her ministries that uplifts women in prison. To Autumn Smith, these women are not their crimes; they are her "girls," loved, prayed for, respected for who they are as women and as God's creation. Their identity is their potential.

Just like these women, people who interact with Autumn through personal life, business, or her writing, experience being seen—not through the bars that imprison but through the eyes of God, directly into the heart, landing on their greatest potential. That is my desire for all of you.

As you read through the pages of this work, know you have been prayed for, thought of, and valued. With a heart of gratitude, my prayer is that as you read, you too will be left with a liberating fingerprint on your soul that only my sister can provide.

Gracious words are like a honeycomb,
sweetness to the soul and health to the body.
Proverbs 16:24 ESV

Kristen Carter

Founder and Editor in Chief

Taste and See Magazine

Preface

More than anything else this past year, I have learned the importance of community. The Covid-19 pandemic was just the beginning ...

In many respects, I was blessed through the experience. I had an established business, but I quickly found that to keep it, I had to become innovative. This pressure activated a part of me that has been idle for some time, and before long I was full throttle into what felt like building an entirely new business structure. I could no longer travel or stand before large groups, as these things were prohibited, but my message of encouragement was still important, still vital, and still relevant. It still deserved to be delivered. So, I got creative. More and more I provided online sessions and utilized social media. It worked!

What worked the best, though, was realizing that I desperately needed community. I learned very quickly how much I needed my team. Although it was nearly a year before I was able to feel safe about seeing my brother, I spoke to him more than ever. I called my Aunt Kathy and Uncle Jerry, whom I love dearly but had failed to keep in contact with. I texted my best friend from high school and had the opportunity to talk with my favorite junior high science teacher on my birthday.

I learned a lot about myself during the past year. I learned that stretchy pants are a comfort during quarantine but a sneaky deceiver. Ugh! The first time I had to put on real pants after being at home for three months … well, I learned that my stylist is a hero, my dog is an angel, and my clothes shrink with mysterious ease. While cooking at home, I learned not to take a shower when waiting for something to cook. Trust me, you'll end up falling as you rush to the kitchen to silence the timer and the smoke detector all at the same time. And don't forget two very important things as you instinctively open the door to usher out the smoke. One, you are wearing a towel and the neighbors … oh, the neighbors! And two, the alarm is on so you must also combat that startling sound, all while your dog stares at you with contempt and judgment.

So maybe prospering doesn't look much different from a year ago. But one thing looks very different. My peeps! They look different because they are closer to me. I am closer to them. I am humbled as I recognize the need to unify with others. As I was writing *Prospering*, I was learning to trust myself. In writing this book, I am learning to trust others.

One thing that remains the same is that I trust God. My faith in Him keeps me centered and helps me find humor and receive grace. God's love is consistent and fundamental in accepting myself as I am. I love what Mark R. McMinn states in his book *Psychology, Theology, and Spirituality*: "We no longer have to shrink in shame or pretend we are perfectly good, because we are profoundly loved instead."[1]

So please join me once more as I reflect on the beautiful chaos that was 2020 and a bit beyond.

---

[1] Mark R. McMinn, *Psychology, Theology, and Spirituality* (Carol Stream, IL: Tyndale, 2011), 242.

Chapter 1

———◆▸◂◆———

CHEVY

I shivered as I got out of my car to get gas. The wind hit me sharply, and my hair began its usual rebellion against the bun I had secured moments before. I hugged my light sweater against the red wrap dress I was wearing. My beige high heels did little to keep my feet warm. I was about to spend the next several moments considering a more fuel-efficient vehicle until two men caught my attention. They were arguing.

I looked away. Because of situations in my past, hostility—especially with men—terrify me. I have learned to keep to myself. So in this moment, I looked at the gas pump, silently willing it to hurry. But then I caught something out of the corner of my eye. One man had a gun, and his hand had grazed it but reconsidered. Without much thought, I approached the men. I looked at the more masculine one on the left and said, "There is a light on in my dash. You must know more about vehicles than me, and I was wondering if you would look at it."

Both men looked at me in surprise and confusion, but the unarmed man consented. "Sure."

By this time my hair had fallen completely out of the bun, and my cheeks were burning red. We got to the car while the other man left. The gentleman looked in my dash and said, "That just means your door is open." He seemed annoyed, albeit amused. I smiled meekly, thanked the man, and turned to get in my car.

As I was doing so, I put my hair lazily in a defeated ponytail. I felt the man watching me, so I turned around. He was grinning as he said, "You know, I find it very hard to believe that a girl with a Chevy bow tie tattoo on the back of her neck didn't know what that light meant."

I met his gaze and said defiantly, "I didn't say I didn't know. I just asked if you would look at it."

He smiled as he realized what had happened. "Thanks, Chevy." He winked at me knowingly before walking off.

Sometimes we get aggravated with interruptions, criticism, and changes in plans. Even amid chaos, we seldom welcome the unexpected. Maturity happens when we realize that other people see from different angles. They catch things that we miss—things that could hurt us. Other times, it is God who sees things that we don't. We may be arguing, fighting, and jeopardizing our own safety and peace. When God makes a move that we don't understand, we need to trust that it is for our good.

The takeaway here is this. First, I probably should not have become involved in this particular situation. I know this because as I read this draft to a friend, I was met with the same glare I get when I rock climb without a harness or give rides to strangers. It is important to use good judgment. Sometimes, admittedly, I do not.

Second, be thankful for interruptions. Welcome them. They are unavoidable. So instead of investing energy in resisting them, look at them objectively. The very things that we get so worked up about may be directing us in ways that are more beneficial.

Dress warm, trust God, embrace interruptions, and—for goodness' sake—be selective where you stop for gas.

Chapter 2

———◆►◄◆———

LIAR, LIAR

Do faces look different when people lie? I wonder this silently to myself as an associate embellishes on a lie. In one of my classes, they said that people tend to look to the left when they lie and to the right when they are recalling the truth. I never know if it is to their right or my right. I contemplate this as he continues. I listen with borderline amusement as I try to count the times that he blatantly fibs. I lose interest quickly, though, and begin counting his ear hairs instead. In case you are wondering, I counted nine lies before I lost interest and twelve noticeable hairs.

As he concludes, I smile and place the evidence of his betrayal back into my briefcase. For now, it is enough that I have learned something about his character. I am content to be "wise as a serpent and harmless as a dove" (Matthew 10:16 NKJV).

You don't always have to confront others. Although this may seem a little passive-aggressive, you truly don't have to engage in battle. You can use wisdom to determine which fights are worth pursuing and which are a waste of your time. You don't have to give the other person the opportunity to put the blame on you—especially when the prospect of them taking responsibility for their actions is unlikely. People who lie to you easily about silly things will also lie to you about serious things. These folks are dangerous in life and in business. It's OK not to do business with these people, and it's just fine if you don't continue relationships with them either. When someone lies so often that even their truth becomes suspicious, it is not because there is anything wrong with you; it is because they have something in themselves on which they need to work.

I try to exercise grace because to say that I have never stretched the truth *would* be stretching it. But as an adult, particularly as a very busy adult, I don't have time to tell stories. I don't have the energy to keep up with them. Also, my eye has a tendency to twitch when I'm less than honest. In case you are wondering, I'm not sure whether it's the left or the right eye that twitches, or if the twitch pertains to the direction I'm subconsciously glancing in. I've also discovered the hard way that it's better to tell the truth, because the truth will always tell itself eventually. The truth may hurt when a loved one or business associate reveals it at first, but it is always more devastating when it surfaces in a way that is less than direct.

In the situation concerning my associate, I had to ask myself, do I care about this person? Absolutely. Do I care enough about this person to engage in battle? Not so much anymore. Conflict can be good. It means that there are at least two people who care enough about something to go to war. When conflict isn't present, it usually means there is nothing worth fighting for, be it business or personal. So this time I choose just to listen. Business as usual. Do I have the same relationship with him? Of course not, because it is impossible to feel secure when people lie, whether it's something simple like Christmas cards or something serious like professional contracts. It hurts to be lied to. It's that simple.

Can you demand that associates or friends be honest? Nope. Not even most of the time. You can't control other people. You can only control yourself. Being dishonest is sometimes easier on the front end, but it has serious consequences. It can cost you business deals and relationships. It can certainly hurt the people who love you the most. Being honest can be extremely difficult, but it demonstrates a deep respect for the people to whom you tell the truth. It lets them know that you consider them worthy of the truth and capable of handling it. So while we can't demand honesty from other people, we do have the responsibility of being honest with the people we care about and the people we do business with. And men, you also have a responsibility to keep ear hairs trimmed. If you can't be honest, at least be well groomed.

Chapter 3

---◆▸✕◂◆---

UNEXPECTED

I doubt that anyone really expected city offices to be closed, schools to be canceled, or concerts to be postponed. I certainly didn't expect the impact of the coronavirus. It seemed like a far-off circumstance that would never really reach me or my community. Now, businesses are closed in the interest of public safety. I never expected this.

Several of the companies I am contracted with are having difficulty securing materials needed to complete projects. Because they are becoming increasingly unable to complete projects, costs will need to be cut in other areas—perhaps in areas such as consulting, speaking, and coaching. So yes, I am concerned.

That said, it is important to stay positive. First, I am reminded of a time in my life when I first went into business. I had $2,000 and spent a third of it on hiring an attorney to set up my LLC. It was scary, but it was also exciting. I learned to work hard as I trusted in God to provide wisdom for recognizing and seizing opportunities. So this little hiccup, when put into perspective professionally? No worries. I know that God has given me everything I need to build something great or even to rebuild something great if necessary.

I have been eating with associates in restaurants less and eating at home with my family more. The circumstances are not the best, but the opportunity to reconnect with family in this way is not like anything I ever expected. It's nice.

The canceling of client consults was somewhat unexpected, but so too was the extra time available to call and chat with my brother and his family. I've talked to them more in the last two weeks than I have in the last two months.

I've had my first day off in almost two years, and I've spent it exactly as I've always fantasized: at home in my pj's, watching reruns of old sitcoms I enjoyed in high school. I didn't expect a day off, but I've expected very little of what is happening in our world right now. I never know what is next, and if I'm honest, that's a bit unsettling.

It shouldn't take a virus to slow us down and remind us of what matters most, from communicating with our families to practicing good hygiene. It shouldn't take chaos to increase our faith—but sometimes it does, and this time, it has. It appears that the unexpected is becoming the new norm, and people are understandably frightened. It is up to us to educate ourselves, protect our communities, and seize the unexpected opportunities that come with this experience.

This is the perfect time to rest and reconnect with folks in creative ways. This is an ideal moment to clean and organize that spare room in your home. Work a puzzle. Read a book— better yet, read your Bible! Pray. Pray for your family, your friends, your associates, your city, your country, and your whole world. Pray that this will pass quickly. Pray for small businesses. Pray for health-care professionals. Pray for your government. You have unexpected free time, so use it to think of others and lift them up in prayer.

The unexpected can be scary, but it can also be full of potential—potential for personal growth, increased faith, and even improved well-being. Be smart. Be safe. Be inspired.

Chapter 4

———◆—※—◆———

Old Habits

I am not spontaneous. What I am is most certainly a creature of habit. My business grants me all the excitement I can handle and makes it incredibly important that I establish and maintain what little routine my profession allows. Ergo, I take the same exit at least three times a week because when I am able to work in my home state, I always handle my business in the same area of the city. My favorite grocery store is there—yes, I have a favorite grocery store because I am mostly an adult. My usual running route is there. My friends are there. My favorite restaurant and my favorite coffee house are there, beckoning me towards my next visit.

You can understand how I got confused recently when I had local business demands that took me somewhere other than the familiar habitat of Hillcrest. I was busy coordinating schedules with an associate via phone when I realized that I had taken my habitual exit instead of the one I intended to! Instantly, I confronted one-way streets and red lights intent on making me late for my next meeting. I gritted my teeth and wondered, *What is wrong with me?*

As it turns out, nothing is wrong with me. I am human, and for humans breaking old habits is hard. For professionals, responding to criticism, developing new procedures, and adapting to new routines can be difficult too. I have worked diligently for months in the revamping of my business, Autumn Smith Inspires. I have prayed and had others pray with me. I have teamed up with some of the greatest professionals in the industry, and I truly believe that now is the time to relaunch with greater purpose and more focus.

Focus is not easy for me. It takes me no time at all to forget what I'm doing. Keep shiny things out of my office—*please*. And not just shiny objects—keep things that spin away from me too. I don't even have a fancy spinning office chair anymore. I know my limitations, and I adapt to my environment accordingly. That's something we all need to do as professionals. We all should create environments that facilitate focus. Otherwise, we may find ourselves taking familiar exits, missing where we really need to be—and missing opportunities. It would be terrible to forfeit our potential to grow our businesses or improve our relationships when we choose instead to surrender into the security of our familiar old habits.

When God calls us to act and leads us in new and unexpected directions, we must be purposeful in our pursuit to focus on His plan. It's super easy to get distracted by phone calls and scheduling conflicts and take the wrong exit. Our commitment to following Christ's direction needs to be intentional. I like the scripture that says, "No soldier gets entangled in civilian pursuits, since his aim is to please the one who enlisted him" (2 Timothy 2:4 ESV). *Focus.*

As it turns out, I did find my way back on track and made it to my meeting on time. Praise the Lord! But it would have been so much easier had I just paid more attention in the beginning and taken the correct exit first. We will all get distracted from time to time, but let's agree to make a diligent effort to keep our focus on God and His leadership in all areas of our lives, both personal and professional. Trust me, really great things can happen when you break away from old habits and trust God's direction.

Chapter 5

---✦✦✦---

A DAY FOR MY LORD

Is it possible that I can sleep until 7 a.m. without waves of guilt pounding into my consciousness like rapids in Colorado? Not really. But today, I will try. Yesterday a trip was canceled, so I found myself with no clients and no appointments. How did I use this time? I spent the day finishing up end-of-month responsibilities and getting ahead on school assignments for my graduate program. I cleaned places in my home I didn't realize even got dirty. Yes, the microwave should be cleaned more than once every two years. I figured that out while I was scrubbing it yesterday. After cleaning everything and getting office work completed, I found myself in a precarious situation today. I had no work to do. I was experiencing what normal people must feel on Saturday mornings, except it was Wednesday.

I must confess, the stillness was a bit unnerving. I truly didn't know what to do with myself. I called my brother, but he was as work. Another rush of guilt crashed against the shore that is my mind as I again realized that while he was at work, I still was not. I looked at my dog, who looked back at me in confusion. I wonder whether he was a little shaken too, as his routine was disrupted as well. Was he also thinking that we should be in the office right now? I take a deep breath. I am OK. This is

OK. Normal people do this. Normal people take breaks. I sip my coffee and read my Bible. I ask God to bless this day.

I scheduled a massage! I went in and chatted to God in my thoughts the whole time I was getting the massage. At first, I talked to God about my shortcomings as I completed a mental checklist of my discretions and asked for forgiveness. With that business taken care of, I then directed my focus to my actual business. I asked God to bless my work. From there the mental conversations jumped around to everything from my family and friends to the stray cat I have been working diligently to befriend.

After the massage, I went for a walk. It was wonderful! I continued to talk to God. Someone recently asked me how I hear God speak. Well, for me it's a little different. He speaks to me through scriptures, but also I hear words without hearing words. It's more of a knowing. I know the words without audibly hearing them. It's difficult to explain because it's holy, and holy things are sometimes difficult to capture in words. I believe that God speaks to everyone in ways that are unique to each person. That is one of my favorite things about God. He loves us as individuals. At one point during the walk, I promise I felt the words as God told me a joke about birds. I'm not kidding. It was real, and I smiled at how much God loves me and how much I feel that love when I slow down and spend time with Him.

From there I went home and worked peacefully in my garden. I continued to talk to God. I asked Him to bless my garden and help my plants to grow. I asked Him to bless my home. I rattled and I listened. I sang praises to Him as I weeded my onions, okra, and tomatoes. That evening, I settled in with a

AUTUMN SMITH

book about God's grace, and I felt indescribable peace as I read. I ended my day with overwhelming gratitude.

Today I did not sign any important contracts nor make any big deals. I didn't awe an audience or mark off impossible to-do lists. Today I spent time in the presence of my God. I allowed Him to renew my heart and restore my peace. Today was beautiful.

Return, O my soul, to your rest;
for the LORD has dealt bountifully with you.
Psalm 116:7 ESV

Chapter 6

———◆►✖◄◆———

FRIENDS AND BUSINESS

"I have to let her go." These words hung in my throat even as I said them. I did not want to let my contractor go. She had become a friend, and I adore her. I continue, "She has just become so unreliable." I'm on the phone with the man I have come to love and trust as a father, but I feel that I may be speaking more to my impatient heart or maybe even to God—George just happened to be on the phone, overhearing the dialogue as I sorted through my thoughts out loud.

I just feel the frustration of days without communication comingling with the anxiety building about the parts of my business I entrust to her. I must consider that I do trust her, and that is rare for me, especially with my business. Could I ever find someone to replace her that I could trust? I know I am talking more to God at this point.

I received a text and an explanation the next day. She is a beautiful person, and like me, she suffers from anxiety. Situations overwhelm her, and she had experienced another catastrophe. We talked. We prayed. We continued working together. Truly "love covers a multitude of sins" (1 Peter 4:7 ESV).

As important as my business is to me, sometimes I need to slow down and realize that the people who make my work worthwhile are truly what is important. My clients and my associates are amazing. They are human, but then again so am I, and they deal with me. I am grateful.

Chapter 7

---◆▶◀◆---

FOUR MORE STEPS

I found myself lost after teaching one of my sessions at the jail. As I was wandering to the exit, nothing looked familiar. I began to panic. I walked what felt like a million miles as my heart started racing. I started to perspire and felt short of breath. That environment is never a comfortable one to begin with, but under pressure, wow ... just wow. I didn't see any guards. The only ones I passed in the hallway were male trustees. I smiled at the irony of almost instinctively asking them how to get out, although my humor in that moment was only mildly amusing even to me.

Finally, I passed a glass door and thought I saw someone in uniform move behind it. Nope. I tapped on the glass, wondering how very suspicious I must look. No one acknowledged me, so I thought, *I'll just walk a little bit farther.* Within literally three or four steps, I was at the exit and passing the guards, only to hear them laughing as they watched me on the surveillance cameras, aimlessly wandering like a mouse in a maze. "You come here every Friday," they mercilessly reminded me. I sighed a defeated sigh. *I just need to lay down, I need a nap.*

I was so shaken from the experience that I put my address into the GPS of my car—at this point, I had come to doubt my navigational ability even enough to find my way home. I called my sister, Kristen, and told her what happened. She laughed too, but her laughter is like the laughter of baby angels. Unlike the mockery of the guards, who have never been very friendly to me anyways, Kristen's laugh soothed me. In the guards' defense, their experience has probably made them a bit weary and skeptical of everyone. Truth be told, they are good at their jobs, and I appreciate them.

What can I learn from this horridly embarrassing situation? First, obviously, pay attention. Second, don't become overconfident in methods and routines. The wrong paths look eerily similar to the one you're supposed to be on but before you know it, nothing looks familiar. Third, keep going. I was four steps from where I needed to be. Had I succumbed to my fear and retreated to the fetal position in sobs instead of just taking a few more steps in the hallway, I don't think I could even begin to write about the experience. I would probably still be there crying in despair! Fourth, if you find yourself on the wrong path and manage to get back on track, you sometimes need to be extra diligent not to get lost again. Use your resources—your Bible, your support systems, your GPS, whatever it takes to stay the course.

When scripture encourages us to "be still" (Psalm 46:10), I think that means "be at peace." Be calm. Be steady. Be diligent. I may be wrong, but had I literally been still, I'd still be lost. I don't believe God wants us to stay in circumstances which He graciously gives us the "power and self-control" (2 Timothy 1:7 ESV) to remove ourselves from. God doesn't want us to remain lost in our circumstances, and certainly not in our sins.

The stillness I feel that God wants for us is the stillness of our spirits as we move according to His will. Though chaos abounds around us, we can experience peace as we take the next one, two, three, or even four steps to freedom. Keep moving.

Chapter 8

———◆━━◆◆◆◆━━◆———

BETTER INSTEAD

"Ouch!" I let out a not so subtle scream from the kitchen.

A mildly concerned voice responded from the next room. "Are you OK? What happened?"

"I cut my finger."

"Is it bleeding?"

I assessed the injury and responded honestly, "Yes, if I squish it."

A not so amused voice responded, "Well, don't squish it."

Silence. I squished it.

And this sums up my life. I make mistakes. I become anxious. I worry a lot. As if that is not bad enough, then I squish it. To make it worse, I usually squish it after I talk to God about it. "God, I've really messed up this time."

"Is it bad?"

"Yes, if I squish it."

"Don't squish it."

Silence. I squish it.

It must be in my nature to make bad situations worse even though I'd love to make things better instead. The amazing thing, though, is what happens even after I make it worse. Someone comes to the kitchen, washes my cut finger, reassures me, and instructs me how to put the knives in the dishwasher with the sharp edge down. That is mercy. Mercy is when God looks upon us and knows our hearts. God sees our messes and self-induced injuries and cares for us, lovingly directs us away from the source of our pain and disobedience, and shows us a better way—His way.

Two days later, my cut finger still hurts a little, but I have not repeated the offense. As it turns out, we are not exempt from the consequences of our sins. But with a little corrective discipline and loving guidance, we have what we need to avoid the situations and traps that have ensnared us in the past. Will I get careless and put the knives in wrong again? Yes, probably. Will I cut myself and squish it? I really want to say no, but ...

God's grace is not an excuse to make poor decisions. Cut fingers still hurt. Squished cuts still bleed. God doesn't want this kind of life for us. He wants us to have life and have it more abundantly (John 10:10)! But when we do get careless, God will take care of us. His grace is sufficient, and nothing can separate us from His love (Romans 8:38–39). It is because of this love that we endeavor not to mess up or make our messes worse. His love motivates us to do good—to honor Him. Our efforts, though, are not enough to reconcile us to God or to clean up our messes. Only through the blood of Christ are we restored to right standing before God (Ephesians 1:7–10).

Do I still feel silly for cutting my finger? Yeah, a little bit. Does my embarrassment change anything? No. In the same way, carrying guilt for something that God has already forgiven is without purpose and hinders our service to God and to others. Accept God's forgiveness. Instead of beating yourself up or squishing injuries, rest securely in God's protection and grace. He's more than a Band-Aid that covers the cut. He is the healer, the great physician (Luke 5:31). The cut isn't covered, it's gone! There is therefore no condemnation (Romans 8:1).

Be kind to yourself. God has offered forgiveness. Receive it. The condemnation we continue to carry after Christ has already justified us is just another way of squishing a situation and making it worse. Allow God to be God. Accept His goodness and His grace. Let go of the shame and the guilt and the anger you've been carrying for so long. Isn't it heavy? Aren't you tired? I know that I am exhausted.

I will pray for you, and I ask with all sincerity that you continue to pray for me. I accept forgiveness, and I relinquish guilt. Today I am moving forward with my life. Please, you are loved and life is big, so move forward too. Today let's allow God to make things better instead.

Chapter 9

————◆✕◆————

LESSONS

Like a scene from a sci-fi movie, I enter the grocery store as a number. Number 39. I am greeted by someone whose job is to keep up with my number and know when I enter and exit so that the next civilian can be granted access.

I am reminded by a pleasant yet robotic voice echoing through the intercom, "Welcome, valued shopper. Please maintain a social distance of at least six feet between you and the other shoppers. This is for your safety. Please comply. Have a nice day."

I see masks and frantic people desperately trying to secure necessary items. I see an older lady unable to find toilet paper. It is survival of the fittest when it comes to items once taken for granted. It seems I am the only one to notice her. Where am I?

People look at one another in the same way shelter dogs look through their cages—longing for attention but unable to interact. There is a deep longing in the way we make eye contact and quickly look away. It seems unreal, and yet it is real. But for how long? We don't know.

Wasn't it just a month ago that we complained about going to work so early? Now many of us no longer have jobs. Those of us who do are working from home. Maybe the irritating associate or coworker really isn't so bad. We should give him or her a call. We want to talk and to connect with someone. Anyone.

I personally have always hated shopping. Now I make an extra lap around the grocery store, rushed only by the thought of eager shoppers waiting outside to take my number. Church services that once seemed inconvenient are now something I miss deeply. Dinners and gatherings that I once fought to get out of now seem like something to treasure. I regret the time I didn't take to visit home more often.

And yet I am more deeply connected to my family than ever. I listen more attentively, and I talk with more enthusiasm because those interactions are so precious to me now. There are lessons to be learned through this experience.

Things that seemed important are not as vital as I thought. And things that I failed to make time for in the past have become things to cherish in the last few weeks. I am thankful for my health and for the health of my family. I am grateful for my home. I am thankful for my faith. I am thankful that although my flesh is given to fear, my spirit, having been made in the image of God, is not afraid of anything that can merely destroy the body and not the soul (Genesis 1:27; Matthew 10:28). My spirit is eternal.

Yes, there are lessons to be learned from this experience. Lesson one: introverts are only weird when there's not a crisis. We are like superheroes. When a crisis breaks lose, our capes (and masks!) come out. I've learned that I should never *ever* cut my own hair or my dog's based on knowledge acquired through YouTube videos.

I cannot shape my own eyebrows despite what Pinterest would have me believe, and I will tip my pedicurist more generously in the future. I have learned that my dog is capable of deep theological conversations but incapable of picking up his own messes.

I have learned that you can run out of funny animal videos, and you probably will not use extra time as productively as you have always imagined. You cannot learn Spanish in a day, and if you decide to make tomato cages for the first time, also be prepared to get a tetanus shot. When making rolls, do not become impatient. Wood paint does not paint metal well, and it's not a good idea to name opossums that show up in your backyard.

I have learned that going out in public seems like living out a futuristic sci-fi novel. Going home seems like stepping back in time, and there really is no place I'd rather be than in the moment—regardless of what that moment feels like. It is good to be alive. We don't know what the future will bring, and we can't go "back" to normal because "normal" is impossible now.

Things are different. We have today. We have right now, and what we have right now can be scary and beautiful, chaotic and wonderful. We will see what we are looking for, so let's look at one another and see the good even when it is buried deep inside the burden of uncertainty.

We can look for obstacles, or we can look for and find opportunities to make the beauty easier for others to see. This isn't a novel or a movie. This is life, and there are lessons—hard lessons. Lessons that teach us a lot about ourselves. So let's live humbly, seek wisdom, and apply truths to our actions. Be safe. Be blessed. Be grateful.

Chapter 10

---◆➤✦◆---

LIKE A BOSS

I think you fully realize you are a grown-up when a thirteen-year-old child tells you, "You don't know how to have fun." You absolutely know that you are a grown-up when your instinctive reply is, "Whatever. I'll have you know I have a puzzle I intend to work—one thousand pieces!" And as if there were any doubt remaining, you really, really know you are a grown-up when you fall asleep at 8:30 and never even get the puzzle out of the box. I'm not exactly "adulting" like a boss.

Sometimes, I chase the squirrels running loose in my best friend's head or get lost on roundabouts. Seriously, how many roundabouts does one city need? If you plan on visiting Conway, Arkansas, you are in for a treat—roundabouts are everywhere. In these moments, I am adulting even less like a boss.

It's astounding how I can go from running a successful company to losing my phone while I'm talking on it. Or how I can run ten miles for fun but waste twenty minutes trying to find the closest parking spot at the grocery store. Other things are more complicated, like how I can bite my tongue in a board meeting but lose my temper at home, make time for solitaire but not for exercise, or rant to thirty people about a bad experience instead of talking to God about it once.

Some days, I feel like I have the role of being an adult down to a science—everything makes sense. My work is productive, and my relationships are rewarding. Other days, anything from the gas pump to the coffee barista can frustrate my agenda. I find that most days fall somewhere in between. Somedays, I am so spiritual and thank God for my salvation, my family, and my home. Today, I thanked Him for dry shampoo.

It's a great feeling to have your act together, but the most wonderful thing is to know that even when you don't, God still accepts you. When you're kneeling at the altar or crying out to Him from your car, He hears you. Whether you're asking for leadership in your ministry or your way out of a new roundabout, He hears you. Whether you are confessing or rejoicing, He hears you.

God wants you when you are adulting like a boss—or a little less like a boss. It's not the moment or the mood you're in that matters. His affection for you is not situational; it's consistent, and it's eternal. "See what kind of love the Father has given to us, that we should be called children of God; and *so we are*" (1 John 3:1 ESV, my emphasis). Scripture doesn't say "so we are" until we mess up or cry because the delivery guy brought us the wrong pizza. It says "and so we *are*," present tense.

While we may change from minute to minute, God remains the same. He doesn't change His mind about us: "Jesus Christ is the same yesterday and today and forever" (Hebrews 13:8 ESV). He loves us unconditionally and irrevocably.

So relax. We're not called to adult like a boss or even close to it; we are called to serve God with the unique gifts that He has provided. Some days that looks like a well-rehearsed ballet, and other times it looks like a "Macarena" dance in the kitchen, trying to catch flying spatulas. So whether you feel like a boss or a little less like a boss, you are incredibly loved either way.

Chapter 11

<hr>

NEW ADVENTURES

I stare into the backseat of my car, curious as to how my dog, Oscar, is going to respond to this new adventure! In nearly ten years, Oscar, although a rescue, has demonstrated zero fear in response to anything. I sit straight up in my bed, alarmed on the Fourth of July. The sounds of fireworks late into the night send me straight into full-pledged panic. The only thing louder than the fireworks on this holiday is the sound of Oscar snoring content and cozy in my bed. Thunder does not bother him. When tornado sirens go off, I hold him in the hallway with tears falling down my cheeks while he nestles clumsily in my arms enjoying all the extra snuggles. So now as I put my car into neutral, I worry that what can only be described as a disco car wash will negatively impact his otherwise calm demeanor.

I get nervous, but Oscar rests soundly through the entire experience. The flashing colorful lights do not excite him. He does not even notice the loud noises. Except for a large yawn that hints of frustration that his nap was minimally disrupted, he does not move at all. I envy his position of security. It is not as if he doesn't know the world can be mean; he was abandoned when he was just a puppy. So why is it now that he can rest totally secure while chaos ensues around him? Easy—he has learned to trust me. He knows that I will keep him safe! He has no reason to worry. It occurs to me in this moment, What if I could trust God in His magnificence the way Oscar trusts me in my feebleness?

We look at the world and see things we never expected to see. We look at our careers and become vastly aware of the insecurity of our positions. We look at our culture and find that we are at war within our own communities. We look at our families and our lives, we see our futures and our pasts, and we are rendered terrified. Sure, we have been through a lot. Most of our fears are rooted strongly in our experiences. We fear financial insecurity because we have been without. We fear abandonment because we have felt rejection. Fear is a learned response. and rational or not, fear is in opposition to what God desires from us.

Our fears focus our attention inward on ourselves and our own inability and ineffectiveness to protect ourselves and control our destinies. Control is a myth! So long as we are relying on our own strength, we are failing to acknowledge the sufficiency of Christ, and we are tormented with failure. Bad things will happen: "in the world you will have tribulation. But take heart; I have overcome the world" (John 16:33 ESV).

Our fear is no longer justified because as Christians we know that this world and the damage it causes is temporary. We should trust like Oscar. The tornado is not any less threatening because he refuses to fear it, nor is it any more threatening because I give all my energy to it. We cannot control the storm.

AUTUMN SMITH

We can control our response to it. We can take steps to protect ourselves: study scripture, pray, and strive to live obedient lives. But when we have done all that we can do, we must stand securely in God's provisions and *trust* that He is working in every new adventure.

Chapter 12

———◆►◄◆———

Puppy Play?!

I have been social distancing for more than a month because of the coronavirus pandemic, and I have gone a little insane. If only my favorite Mexican food restaurant and my hair and nail salons would open back up, perhaps things would be different. But as it is, I am losing my mind.

Ergo, I read an article suggesting that pets could acquire the virus, so I went online. I innocently googled "puppy masks" believing that Oscar and I could procure matching protective gear. You can imagine my horror when something called "puppy play" intruded on my screen! I had no idea what it was. Although I didn't intend to start my day off with pictures of half-naked men wearing puppy tails and—you guessed it— puppy masks, that is exactly what happened. Of course, I didn't click on anything, but wow, was I ever embarrassed anyways …

So there you go. It's that easy. Something innocent can accidentally lead to something obscene, and before you know it, you're calling your best friend to tell her that you may have accidentally watched pornography. You are fully convinced that Google believes you to be a pervert. Needless to say, I was devastated.

I think the greatest feeling in the world is learning something one day that you didn't know the day before. But today I am overwhelmed by the fear of "what if I only get to learn one new thing a day?" What if I wasted my "one new thing" on something called puppy play?!

In a panic, I think I can erase the experience by intentionally learning something new, but no. I will need to consult an encyclopedia to learn my next new thing. Because if I get only six accidentally naughty searches before Google flags me as dirty, I cannot risk another flag in the same day. I only have four left because of an unfortunate Dr. Seuss incident in 2016. Don't ask. I'm not even sure it works that way, but just in case, I've decided that I will turn my computer off for the rest of the day.

Let's examine my experience as it pertains to sin. Did I sin? I would say no. I didn't look at the pictures or click for further examination. It wasn't a temptation to me at all, and yet I just felt yucky and beat myself up!

We will, however, face temptations in life. We are flesh, and the flesh will sometimes encounter things that bring us to people, substances, and distractions that have the potential to lead us astray. We will feel angry, jealous, and bitter from time to time, but we can't dwell on these things.

We have to consciously make a decision not to "click" on temporal things that pull our attention away from the eternal. The sin is not in being tempted, it's in acting upon those temptations. If I were to google "puppy masks" again knowing what would show up, *that* would be a sin. Rather, we should choose not to "enjoy the fleeting [temporary] pleasures of sin"

(Hebrews 11:25 ESV). We should instead focus on goodness and heavenly virtues.

It seems to me that if Satan cannot cause us harm by enticing us to sin, he then causes us harm by shaming us for being tempted in the first place. Scripture, on the other hand, tells us that to be tempted is not a sin. Jesus was tempted! When Jesus was tempted in the wilderness, the "tempter came and said to him, 'If you are the Son of God, command theses stones to become loaves of bread'" (Matthew 4:3). Jesus had fasted forty days. He was hungry. Yet He did not inquire as to whether the stones would make better wheat, raisin, or rye bread! He didn't entertain the temptation at all. He immediately used scripture to put the devil in his place—a very good reason to learn and memorize scripture.

The truth is that we are drawn away by our "own desire … then desire when it is conceived gives birth to sin, and sin when it is fully grown brings forth death" (James 1:14-15). Temptation should be avoided when possible. Don't put yourself in situations to be tempted. Sometimes that means turning the computer off for the day. Sometimes that means not going where alcohol will be served. It means different things to different people.

But inevitably, we will encounter situations in which we innocently end up on the wrong side of things. And while the devil will tell you that you should feel guilty and shameful, God will tell you to count it a joy in that "the testing of your faith produces steadfastness. And let steadfastness have its full effect, that you may be perfect" (James 1:3–4).

This does not mean that we should become proud when we withstand temptation, for even our righteousness is as rags (Isaiah 64:6). Rather, by withstanding temptation, we have confirmed the work of the Holy Spirit in our lives and demonstrated that we do not live in the flesh but in the Spirit (Galatians 5:25).

Do not become or remain a slave to shame. God offers forgiveness. I heard it said once that God forgives all sins, past, present, and future. All sin was future sin when Jesus died on the cross to redeem us and to restore us to Himself. This gives great hope to believers!

Let us pray that we will not enter into temptation. But when we accidentally Google something we don't expect, let's receive forgiveness and move past it quickly! Let's also remember to be kind to others, because we don't understand the circumstances that led them to destructive decisions—it could have been a series of innocent mistakes.

Let's all be careful what we "click" on!

Chapter 13

———◆◆◆◆———

A Trip Back Home

Some people love to go home. I, on the other hand, sit with feelings of dread in the driver's seat. My head already feels the pangs of a migraine, and something like a brick sits in my stomach. I watch familiar buildings pass through the truck windows, and several of my thoughts become audible against my will. I feel instant guilt as I mutter, "I hate this place." I see paint peeling off once near-pristine buildings downtown, and I sigh. If the buildings could articulate their judgments on my changing appearance, I think they would probably sigh too. Things are eerily familiar, and yet quite different.

I am sad because maybe somewhere in the back of my mind I had hoped things would be better, both in the downtown square and in myself. It was not to be. The small town still seems too exclusive, and I still feel too resentful. I keep driving.

In just fifteen minutes, exactly twelve miles of curvy roads out of town, I would be pulling into my old driveway. I would be passing Granddo's house, and I would land in front of my mother's place, where my brother and his family now reside also.

My childhood was not all bad. There were pockets of poverty, neglect, abuse, and abandonment, but there was also my Granddo. She loved me, and when she passed, I thought that I would never come back to this place. But I did.

Once when I found myself with nowhere to go, Granddo's old home, which had set empty for a few years, welcomed me with shelter for nearly a year until I got back on my feet. And now, my brother has taken up residence there, so I swallow my pride and return every now and again to visit.

My brother loves the place. He points out the beauty in our old family land. It's true. The mountains are beautiful, and there was a time I enjoyed running through the woods, climbing trees, and building forts. The church near our family home was nice too. The church folks were some of the best around. I won't say that I got an ideal education in our rural school, where I graduated with nine other students, but the teachers cared deeply about us. It's an honor to say that I am still in contact with a few of the best. Truth be told, people in our small community continue to be incredibly supportive of my work and success. When I think about it, there were more good people than bad. I feel guilty that my mind and my mouth sometimes clump them all together.

I am reflective as I smell smoke coming off the grill and watch my big brother make fun of me as he grills me a veggie burger instead of the beef that he cooks for everyone else. He's a good sport. I look to my left and see my young niece on her makeshift tree swing and smile at her youth. She is beautiful, and for a moment I am grateful that she is getting to grow up in this place.

After visiting for the afternoon, I leave lost in confusing feelings that I decide not to fully process just yet. I know that may not be the healthiest decision, but for now I just want to get back to my home and rest.

Later I realized I was exhausted from already trying to decide how I felt in any given moment. I think mostly I felt joy—I was enjoying home until thoughts crept back in about the hurt I had experienced there years before. The past tried diligently to rob me of the present joy. I had to wrestle myself back into the moment where I was enjoying my family. Overall, I felt I had defeated the past, but I was tired. I had won, but the victory had taken its toll on me.

I think our pasts can be good or bad, and mostly a little of both. I'm not sure why I sometimes feel that I can't experience more than one at the same time. I think dual emotions are natural. Roses have thorns, after all. The rose no more takes away the danger of the thorns than the thorns have the power to take away the beauty from the rose. I'm not a poser for enjoying a day where I grew up, and I'm not a hypocrite for dreading it. Our pasts carry a combination of heavy potentials.

It's OK to dread things that evoke hurtful memories, and it is very much OK to enjoy the enjoyable moments, even if it's in the same space. Fight to be present. Rest when you need to. We are far more critical of our thoughts than others would be if they knew our story. So be kind to yourself.

Chapter 14

———◆◆◆———

DONUTS!

Everyone should know that I love donuts! I especially love the long donuts glazed with chocolate and filled with creamy sugary goodness. I'm not really sure exactly how to go about ordering them because when I was growing up, we called them "long johns." The sweet older woman who owns and operates the local bakery I enjoy does not speak English well, and she looks at me like I'm pulling an inappropriate eighth-grade prank when I call them that. Believe me, trying to describe them does not make it better—you can imagine.

Anyhow, Thursday morning I ordered one successfully, but as the sweet lady started to hand me the goods, she looked disappointed. "They seem to have overfilled your donut," she explained. "Would you like me to make you another one?"

As I tried to wrap my head around the idea that overfilling a donut was even a possibility, I tried to hide my enthusiasm. "No thank you," I replied meekly. "I'll manage."

It was amazing—the gooey goodness squished out both ends with every bite! I called three people who couldn't believe my good fortune. OK, so maybe they weren't as excited about the donut thing as I was, but they all politely congratulated me, and I received their acknowledgments with the same eagerness as I gobbled down my delicious treat.

The truth is, there will be things that happen in your life that people won't be able to share from your perspective. The same donut that the baker saw as a failure, and a few other folks felt indifferently about, was *spectacular* to me. Seriously, it made my entire day.

Sometimes people look at other people that way too. It's really all about perspective. And here's the amazing thing: *you* get to choose your perspective. You get to decide if the donut is worth celebrating. Other people don't get to decide what you see in the mirror. You do. If someone is indifferent about your new job or discourages your business venture, that's OK … how does it feel to you? What is God telling you about the donut? If He is telling you that you're blessed, then trust Him!

I am grateful for many things, some serious and some silly. I am grateful that each day I can celebrate things that make me happy. I pray that today and for always you choose joy.

Chapter 15

❖◀✖▶❖

MAKEUP

I hate makeup. There, I said it.

Sure, I put it on, and I think I clean up pretty good, but I really hate doing it. Some women love it, and that's great. I wish I did, but I don't. I hate paying for it. I hate applying it. I hate taking it off at night. It's just one more step in a skin care regimen that I resent. When I do shows, someone usually does my makeup for me, and that's when it really looks amazing. Unfortunately, when I do it myself … well, let's just be honest. I usually don't do it at all when I must do it myself. It really annoys me! I feel funny even confessing it because it's so ridiculous.

My mom used to spend hours every morning "putting her face on." She's beautiful. She also took it to the next level with matching outfits and coordinating jewelry. What a woman! I, on the other hand, remember being a kid and wondering why she did that when she could've been doing something fun like catching crawdads or building forts. I was wadding my tangled hair up in messy buns before it was cool and running out the door barefoot in cutoff shorts to dig up worms. While she was getting "made-up," I was getting in trouble for messing up my Sunday dress. Not a lot has changed.

A lot of folks see me doing what I do. I love what I do. I don't even mind getting "made-up" for my work. It's the equivalent of paperwork in jobs that professionals in other industries otherwise enjoy. It's a necessary evil to make possible something amazing. However, if you were to come to my home, you would most likely find me in a pair of sweatpants, an oversized T-shirt, no makeup, and a messy bun. That is me. It's no more real or unreal than my stage persona; it's simply another side of me—a more comfortable side.

What we tend to do as professionals is assume that people are only as they show us they are. We assume the take-charge, type-A boss must be impossible to live with. How often have we heard the watercooler gossip to the tune of "his poor wife!" We assume the extroverted associate is energized by a crowd when in fact he is exhausted from wearing his "work face" for twelve hours. We believe the happy-go-lucky intern to be happy indeed. We spend our lives trusting that what we are seeing is the whole picture, yet we miss so much!

Maybe we're lazy. Maybe it's easier to apply makeup than to let ourselves be vulnerable. Maybe it's easier to see other people's makeup at, pun intended, face value. In one scenario, we avoid revealing and working on ourselves. In the other, we avoid the effort it takes to deeply know and care about someone else. We live in a world that loves makeup and make-believe, but there are other sides to every face. There's a side that isn't contoured, bronzed, or highlighted. When will we understand that the face that isn't airbrushed is beautiful too?

The next time you start to roll your eyes at coworkers or behind the boss's back, or to snap back at associates, stop and take a really good look. Take a look beyond the surface, beyond their behavior, beyond your instinctive view. Take a look into the deeper person and try to understand that there is a story there that you know nothing about. There is something that wakes them up at night. They've probably laughed so hard they've cried or cried so hard they thought they might die.

We are not that different from one another if we really look—but that takes effort. It takes effort to look deeper into someone's life, but that's what it takes to be effective. And if you can't make this effort, then you are probably part of the reason they put makeup on in the first place. Isn't that why we all dress up and play pretend—because we fear rejection? Don't we believe that if we are open and honest, people won't respect us or won't like us? Maybe, just maybe, we've been hurt so often that we put makeup on to deceive ourselves. What if we don't like our own reflection?

I struggled with my team during one of the most personally difficult months of my life. I pretended everything was fine. But as I put on what I thought was a fine performance, my crew noticed that I was losing things, forgetting appointments, and despite my best efforts becoming a little more irritable than normal. Gradually, I began to sense that they were losing confidence in my leadership.

So I went into the team meeting with no makeup—literally no makeup. I was wearing jeans and a T-shirt. I was honest. "Look, you all are important to me, so I want to be honest. I am going through a divorce. I am devastated and questioning a lot about myself. I am in a weird place emotionally, and I really need more support than usual on this upcoming campaign." It was like a dose of medicine that you know is working because it burns. It was difficult, but my team huddled around me with so much support and encouragement. They took off some of their own makeup too.

Now, I know that a lot of professional consultants would disagree with me. That's OK. There have to be boundaries in what you share and don't share in professional settings. While it's OK to share that you are in the midst of battle, it's usually best not to share details. That's too much. But from a personal perspective, I find that being honest with the people you entrust your business to is important. My team needs to be able to trust me and a huge part of that trust is made possible because I am transparent with them.

When you consider that most professionals spend more waking hours with their team than they do with their families, it is even more important to occasionally take the makeup off. Otherwise, you run the risk of morphing permanently into your career alias, and there are real dangers associated with becoming one-dimensional.

Seeing and being seen for *all* that we are is a deliberate commitment to being kind to ourselves and to others. It's saying in essence that we are good enough, we are approved of, and we are accepted exactly as we are in every arena of our lives. Makeup has its place, but let's keep it on our faces and not our hearts. Let's agree to be human and to see humans. The illusion of being perfect carries with it expectations that will inevitably lead to far too much pressure and unnecessary disappointment. Today, let's just all decide to be real. Keep makeup to a minimum, please.

Chapter 16

FAST BOATS

I clutched the arm of the person to my right and to my left with fierce survival instincts as I screamed obscenities into the air. The boat sped faster, and I felt tears stinging from my eyes and mixing mercilessly with the cold water from Lake Fort. Finally, when the boat slowed to a stop and I had apologized to my friends for my potty mouth, I got my bearings about me and waited to be shown how to fish for crappie.

No one caught much, but I didn't catch anything. I was too busy thinking about how God had calmed storms and walked on water. That He was a fisherman too. He was successful without fast boats and gadgets, and I'd rather fish that way. How much water there was, and how Noah must have felt during the flood. I managed to get one bite on my line, but I was so lost in my thoughts that it startled me, and I jerked only to lose the fish. Oh well …

I did, however, enjoy the company, and the birds that played over the open water were fun to watch. I did not like the boat or the wind that I was told hampered the fish from biting. When we gave up on fishing, I managed to make it back to the boat ramp without crying. I closed my eyes and thanked God for everything I was thankful for in the day, and I was mostly calm.

I grew up in the hills of rural north Arkansas, and needless to say, hillbillies don't fish that way! We fish from pond banks, which I did with much more success after I returned to the cabin my friend was gracious to let me stay in. Yes indeed, I was much happier on the pond bank, reeling in bass!

I think it's easy to get caught up in comparisons. We would like to teach at bigger churches. We would like to have a music ministry instead of a call to speaking. We are envious of those with gifts that are different from our own. My brother is happy to live a life quietly with his family on the land we grew up on. I, on the other hand, always felt called to the city, or to be no more than a short drive from it. In a way, I am really blessed to have had the opportunity to be raised in the country and now to reside in town. I feel I've had the opportunity to experience the good and bad of both. I'd say I'm well rounded.

In life it's always good to try new things, especially with people you trust. That's how you learn about yourself and your purpose. I bet a lot of folks climb on fast boats, fish for crappie one time, and find themselves hooked (pun intended). Fishing from a pond bank probably just isn't very exciting for most people, but I love it. Soon we must learn that it's great to grow and develop in new and exciting ways, but it's also important to acknowledge where we came from and how it shapes us. It's important to fish in the businesses and ministries you are called to.

I would love to be the girl who loves fast boats and fishing for crappie. But that's not me, and who I am is how God designed me. I'm finally OK with the woman I am, the woman who prefers peaceful pond banks. I pray that you always allow yourselves opportunities that direct you to your true purpose in Christ or reaffirm that you are exactly where you are meant to be. I pray that you are blessed with adventure, and when the adventure passes, I pray that you have peace.

And he said to them, "Follow me, and I will make you
fishers of men." Immediately they left their nets
and followed him.
Matthew 4:19–20 ESV

Chapter 17

---◆───

LABELS

Once or twice each week on my commute, I drive past a house that can barely be seen because the yard is overgrown. I can't help but wonder how this previously well-manicured lawn became such a mess. As I was driving today, I was also chatting to my associate on the phone. I casually glanced at the yard and noticed a very pretty older lady working to restore the lawn to its former pristine condition.

I interrupted the conversation with my associate without hanging up. "Excuse me, can you hold on for just a minute?" With his compliance, I rolled down my window and slowed to a stop to speak to the lady. "What you are doing looks so good!"

She smiled, and as soon as she did, I realized she was stunning. Her eyes matched her silver hair, and I could not believe how beautiful she was when she casually brushed the sweat from her forehead. She told me that she was helping to fix the place up for her son because he had experienced medical problems. I could tell she was enjoying the work. She absolutely glowed at the compliment regarding her efforts.

When I resumed the phone conversation with my associate, he was laughing. "You are the most extroverted introvert in the world!" he exclaimed. I let that sink in because, as is true of most introverts, I am reflective. I considered another incident earlier in the day as I began to confirm his appraisal of my personality.

I had received a call from a telemarketer, and after just ten minutes, I knew his name; the names, breeds, and grooming preferences of his three dogs; and how he and his family planned to vacation once they were able to do so. Although he did not make a sale or learn anything about me, I was glad I was able to make him smile for a few minutes. I thoroughly enjoyed learning a bit about the stranger who, like us all, was just trying to make a living.

It may seem that I am an extrovert. I speak for a living, so it's a reasonable assumption. To the few people who know me well or who have had the awkward experience of seeing me in crowds in which I am not working, it is clear that I am in fact very bashful!

My friends have to beg me out of the house for social interactions. I prefer picking up dinner and taking it home to eating out. But when I do eat out, I will know the names of and other fun facts about the wait staff before I leave.

I believe everyone has a really cool story, and I love to hear them all. Yet I also feel blessed when I can just ride with someone, and they run in and pick up dinner while I wait in the car. Sometimes I enjoy working from coffee houses, because it's revitalizing to be around a group of people and not necessarily be expected to interact. Really, I am that shy.

You see, every interaction is intentional and purposeful for me. If you invite me to coffee or dinner or lunch and I accept, it is because I value you enough to step out of my comfort zone. I believe you are worth it. If I don't know you and I choose to compliment you or your work, it is because I mean it. I think what you do is important, and your work is incredible.

If I stand in front of groups of two to twenty-five people and teach time management, conflict management, or organizational systems, it is because I believe these groups have what it takes to be successful, and I can help. If I stand in front of hundreds to motivate and inspire, it's because I know that someone in that crowd needs what I have to offer.

Introverts would not talk to as many strangers as I do in a day. Extroverts would not seek the comfort of solidarity regularly. I do both of these things! This contradiction eventually led me to an internal conflict that frustrated the introspective introvert of myself and caused the extrovert in me to roll her eyes.

You see, the world tells me that I am extroverted. I tell myself that I am introverted. But the truth is, all that I am is fearfully and wonderfully made, just the way that my God intended me to be (Psalm 139:14). Although I am very shy, I am also an encourager (Romans 12:6–8)—a combination only God could create that suits me perfectly for my purpose to serve and honor Him in a unique way.

The point I'm making is that it is easy to accept labels, assign labels, try desperately to detach from labels—but even harder to live up to them. It's exhausting. We spend a significant part of our time defining ourselves by how other people see us, and they spend a significant part of their energies seeing us through filtered lenses that reflect our actions. Let's be honest, we sometimes do the same to them, and it isn't fair.

It may seem natural to let our actions define us, and in a sense, our actions do stem from our beliefs and circumstances. But even the best of us make mistakes. No one is perfect, and I certainly would hate to carry the labels that I have shamefully earned in my past. It's OK; I don't have to. God has created a clean heart in me, and I am a new creation (2 Corinthians 5:17).

As humans, we can't escape from our tendency to examine, accept, or reject labels. But as Christians, we are given labels that truly fit! Instead of looking to the world or even to ourselves, we can look to the Bible.

God's Word tells me that I am forgiven (1 John 1:9). I am a child of God (John 1:12). I am saved (Romans 10:9), and I am loved (John 3:16). Now those are some labels!

> "Because you are precious in my eyes,
> and honored, and I love you."
> Isaiah 43:4 ESV

Chapter 18

————◆◆◆————

HEAVY LIFTING

"A little on the heavy side," my trainer says as he hands me a set of dumbbells.

I sigh and reply, "Yes, I know. That's why I'm here."

We both laugh knowing he was referring to the dumbbells ... at least I hope he was referring to the dumbbells!

The truth is, I didn't feel like working out today. Emotionally, I was exhausted. I barely felt like getting out of bed, let alone making it up after I finally wrestled my way out of its security. I didn't feel like amusing small talk on the elevator, and I definitely didn't feel like eating breakfast.

Sometimes life is a series of decisions in opposition to what we feel like doing. Feelings are great. They have the potential to alert us to things that need our attention. They connect us to others. They motivate us, they move us, and they can even inspire works of art. Feelings should be acknowledged. The problem with feelings is that they are fleeting, and if not managed, they can create unreasonable chaos—especially when those feelings are a little on the heavy side.

Feelings can overwhelm and confuse us. They can cloud judgment. As believers, we are called to go beyond simply *managing* feelings. We are also accountable for *measuring* them against the truth of God's Word. Feelings will feed thoughts of inadequacy and failure, whereas scripture teaches us that we are fully justified by Christ. We are fully forgiven through His sacrifice. In God's love we are good enough, and to allow our feelings to convince us otherwise is to forfeit the peace that comes through His faithfulness (Romans 5:1–2).

Are our feelings coming from a place of spiritual growth and maturity as we "rejoice with those who rejoice, [and] weep with those who weep" (Romans 12:15), or are we simply entertaining our flesh by failing to "take every thought captive to obey Christ" (2 Corinthians 10:5)? I've found in life that sometimes to be successful, you need to acknowledge your feelings but then wage war against them spiritually. Anyone who has ever suffered at all understands that overcoming "feelings" is nothing less than warfare. Thankfully, God equips us for battle (2 Corinthians 10:3–6).

Some nights you may cry until your eyes burn. You may have nightmares and wake up with a headache. There will be times for mourning (Ecclesiastes 3:4). But there comes a time when you have to do the things that need to be done, regardless of how you feel. Get up. Make your bed. Even if you nearly choke on peanut butter toast and a multivitamin, you will feel nourished after eating. If you have no intention of talking to a stranger on an elevator, do it anyway. You may enjoy their company, and even get some great hair tips! I promise you will feel more energized after a good workout. So a little on the heavy side? No problem. You've got this.

Chapter 19

———◆◆◆———

Too Safe

I won't say that I enjoy mowing the lawn. Mostly, I do not. I think my particular mower is sort of fun to drive, and I like to see the progress as I move along. It's rewarding, albeit a pain in the rump. I could pay someone to do it. But because it's something I *can* do myself, I was raised to believe that I *should* do it myself. So I do.

If you've never seen me mowing the grass, you've really missed something! You see, I like to be safe, and prior incidents have encouraged my due diligence in wearing protective gear to do relatively simple tasks. So as I prepare to mow the grass, I first apply sunscreen. Because I have allergies, I then put on a mask. The mask is complemented with full-coverage safety goggles. Then, to further protect against the sun's brutal rays, I place a ball cap on my head and secure it with noise-reduction safety earmuffs. As you can imagine, I look ridiculous.

Mowing the grass is like being human. We are in the world, and the world can hurt us. We need to be safe. So we are taught to put on the full armor of God (Ephesians 6). Sometimes we think maybe we can get by without the goggles. That is the day we run over a stick that breaks and flies back with uncanny accuracy and strikes us right in the eye! The day we let down our shield is probably the day coworkers approach with the best gossip, or the gorgeous guy down the hall spills coffee on his shirt and *must* take it off right in front of your desk. Don't neglect your spiritual safety gear! Trust me, you'll need it.

One time while I was preparing to mow, I applied sunscreen hastily and ended up with a very irregular burn. Initially I thought the sunscreen had gone bad or lost its effectiveness. Soon, however, I realized the problem was that I didn't apply it correctly.

Sometimes our instinct is to blame the equipment when really it is our application that causes problems and renders us unarmed. Sometimes we take up "the sword of the Spirit, which is the word of God" (Ephesians 6:17 ESV) hastily. Reading the Word becomes something to mark off our to-do list, and we miss the point. Sometimes we misinterpret scripture because we take up the sword without "praying at all times in the Spirit" (Ephesians 6:18). Our study and application of scripture should be intentional and applied with a sincere desire to know God.

It is a fine thing to look at a freshly mowed yard and feel good about it. In fact, scripture tells us that "there is nothing better for a person than that he should eat and drink and find enjoyment in his toil" (Ecclesiastes 2:24). However, scripture goes on to tell us to "fear God and keep His commandments, for this is the whole duty of man" (Ecclesiastes 12:13). Looking at a freshly mowed yard with a black eye and a blotchy sunburn is far less satisfying than looking at a freshly mowed yard injury-free on the back deck in a comfy porch swing.

A yard well mowed is nothing compared to a life well lived. Be diligent in your work. Put on all the armor and all the safety gear. In the spiritual realm, you can't be too safe.

Chapter 20

———◆━◆◆◆━◆———

ANOTHER PERFECT STORM

I pulled a sweater over my shoulders and trembled when the thunder crashed with a majestic intensity that can only be described as something from a Thor movie. I do not like storms, and I was not particularly thrilled with this one even before it rendered my house silent and dark. It was already dark outside, so opening the curtains did nothing to ease the heaviness of the darkness. I scrambled through my house, which suddenly seemed eerie and unfamiliar, in search of a flashlight. I found it, but it would not come on. I reached for my phone to find the battery at less than 10 percent—useless. My dog, recognizing nothing better to do, climbed onto the bed and was asleep within seconds. I, on the other hand, was wide awake.

It was too dark to read. So I finally climbed into bed and surrendered to the circumstances. But I still could not sleep. The silence brought anxious thoughts, and I began to feel the all too common symptoms of a panic attack. The storm outside my bedroom window was nothing compared to the storm raging inside my mind. To recap, it was too dark to read, there was no TV, and there was no phone. I was alone and terrified. So I did what I have been taught to do: I prayed.

It was not the typical prayer of a woman who had her wits about her. It was the desperate pleading of a woman who needed God more than anything. It was almost hysterical. I prayed about theology I had been struggling to understand. I prayed about situations and circumstances. I asked questions with the intensity of Job (Job 7:17–21).

An amazing thing happened when I finally paused. I heard the "sound of a low whisper" (1Kings 19:12), which to me is hard to explain. It is like a quiet but sure "knowing" of the words—not necessarily audible, but very much concrete. I am sure that other people hear Him differently, but this is how I hear God's voice when I listen for it. I experienced this knowing almost immediately with every question I asked. When I finally paused from my inquisition, I sighed and said in my heart, "Wow!" That's when I heard the knowing that responded casually, with almost a hint of humor and a lot of compassion: "What? Did you expect me not to have the answers?" I smiled. I fell asleep peacefully and woke the next morning with my electricity back on. Thank you, Jesus!

I think sometimes that we are so accustomed to being overstimulated with distractions such as our phones and our TVs that it's like an addiction, and we feel lost without these. Even our books and our work can distract us from truly seeking God. Our world is so loud that it will almost take fierce winds that tear through mountains, or earthquakes, or fire (1Kings 19:11–12) to hear God. We miss His voice because we look for it in the storm, when all the storm was meant to do was direct us to Him.

On my own, I would not have put my phone down that night. I would have fallen asleep to the sound of the TV humming in the background. I am guilty of not seeking the Lord as I should. I am so grateful to serve a God that seeks me, the one sheep (Luke 15:3–7). I am so thankful that for a moment, He removed all the distractions competing for my attention and focused my heart on Him. When there was nothing else and no one else, He was there with me. He did not need to calm the storm that night. He needed only to calm me.

Chapter 21

———◆━◆━◆———

ALL I EVER WANTED

I was recently offered and accepted a job that I thought I wanted. In fact, I had prayed specifically for this job. I eagerly wanted to work for someone else and rid myself of the responsibility of running my own business, even if it meant sacrificing the success that came with working for myself. I wanted something "normal," and God gave it to me! It was exactly what I wanted, and I couldn't wait to get started. The offer had come easily as if only from the hand of God. I was thrilled—although something became unsettled in my spirit.

The uneasiness I felt intensified as I got closer to my start date. I prayed, but I also rationalized that this was so specific to my prayer that it had to be God—didn't it? Yes, and no. Let me explain. Yes, because God wanted to teach me something about myself, but no, in that the job wasn't what He had given me as much as the lesson in obedience that came from submitting to His will.

I am thickheaded sometimes, so I rationalized and debated obsessively: is this really God dealing with my spirit, or is this the devil trying to confuse me? First, God is not the author of confusion (1 Corinthians 14:33). He will not create chaos. We create chaos, and the devil plays in it. If it's like a fire, we light the match and the devil throws gas on it. If it's like a flat tire, we chose the wrong road, and the devil puts the nail in our lane, for "each person is lured and enticed by his own desire" (James 1:14 ESV).

Anyway, as I struggled with these feelings, I felt God reveal something to me. My spirit belongs to God. I am His. From the day I accepted Jesus Christ, my soul has been protected. My heart and mind, on the other hand, are very much flesh and therefore a battleground susceptible to attacks from the enemy. If I had been merely struggling with this career decision in my mind or my heart, it would have been very different. As it was, my soul was troubled, and I knew God was asking me to give up what He had provided. My responsibility was not to understand but to accept and act in obedience. I did, and I found peace.

What I had asked for was something to make me happy. It's what *I* wanted. Notice a trend? There was a lot of "me" and "I" in this pursuit. It was a good opportunity with a Christian company, but even good things can be selfish if not pursued in service to Christ and to others. The career was a ministry but not the one that I have been called to.

It is a beautiful thing when we realize that God has called us as individuals. Ministry is not a one-size-fits-all endeavor. All Christians are called to a ministry that they are specifically

AUTUMN SMITH

designed to fulfill. My ministry involves writing, speaking, and coaching. Someone else has a ministry within the food industry or in retail. Whatever we are called to do, let us "work heartily, as for the Lord" (Colossians 3:23).

Oftentimes God gives us what we ask for, but other times He gives us lessons and opportunities to demonstrate obedience. Sometimes, if we are very blessed, God gives us both.

Chapter 22

Upswing

"How are you today?"

An honest question deserves an honest answer, so I reply simply, "Well, I haven't cried since 2 a.m., I accidently got trapped in a parking lot that I couldn't intentionally get out of, and it's almost noon so … I'd say I'm definitely on the upswing!"

The truth is, I am overwhelmed. I am tired. But when I close my eyes, rest does not come. In the place of rest, I experience intense anxiety. When I finally do fall asleep, my dreams are troubled. But that's OK because I will wake up around 2 a.m. with a headache. I will inevitably sit and cry until I become fascinated with an infomercial. I will become convinced that I aspire to be a chef and must have those knives! I will doze back off around 3:30 and be ready for work by 6 a.m.

Clearly, I am not experiencing the fruits of the Spirit! But I am a Christian, so why is this happening to me? Now is the time for some hardcore self-examination. God, search me! It's much easier to surrender to distractions like throwing yourself more heavily into your work; after all, aren't a lot of your anxieties about work? It's also much easier to get lost in an episode of

Guy's Grocery Games on the Food Network than it is to examine scripture late at night. Sometimes, it's easier to cry into a pillow than into the arms of Christ. To cry out to God is to admit that we don't have all the answers, and even though in theory we are humble, it is actually very difficult to accept and confess our inadequacies.

For the last several days, I have avoided a tough conversation with God because I have been living, stressing, and breaking in the flesh. *This is not biblical!* Scripture teaches us that "if we live by the Spirit, let us also keep in step with the Spirit" (Galatians 5:25 ESV). I've been focused on temporal things and neglecting the eternal. Forgive me, Jesus!

> For those who live according to the flesh set their minds on the things of the flesh, but those who live according to the Spirit set their minds on the things of the Spirit. For to set the mind on the flesh is death, but to set the mind on the Spirit is life and peace. (Romans 8:5–6 ESV)

Let's return to the answer I gave to my well-intentioned friend when he asked how I was feeling. Did I really get stuck in a parking lot? Yep! I felt like a mouse in a maze! The harder I tried to find my way out, the trickier the situation became. If I had my Jeep or the truck, I would have driven through the ditch and gotten out of there! However, I was driving my fuel-efficient sedan—and was given a powerful reminder that I am not in control. I finally selected a parking space, put my car in park, lowered my head, and prayed, "God help me with literally everything." And just like that, I lifted my head and saw the exit to this horrible disaster of a parking lot.

Here's the truth. Life can take us to terrible parking lots, and we can drive around in confusion and frustration as we wish for the tools to get out quickly. Only when we realize that we are not in control and that we don't have the necessary drivetrain to get ourselves out of stressful situations do we humble ourselves and let God care for us. Only when we surrender to God can we truly enjoy the fruits of the Spirit, which are "joy, peace, patience" (Galatians 5:22 ESV). I'm glad my friend called when he did because by then I really was on the upswing.

AUTUMN SMITH

Chapter 23

------◆►❈◄◆------

BEING CONTENT

Isn't it just like me to stare at my vegan hot dog with disgust? Not because it is vegan. I am pescatarian (basically a vegetarian except that I occasionally eat fish). You would think that I would be grateful for the variety of options now available to me, but no. Instead of feeling gratitude, I think, *Wow ... vegetarians have it so easy nowadays.* As my good friend and associate put it, "Things are a lot different from when you had to walk uphill three miles both ways in the snow for a veggie burger or carrot!" I hope that you all can appreciate his humor because I fail to see the comic brilliance in his sarcasm.

Nonetheless, he made a valid point. Where once my dietary options were limited, I am now able to enjoy a barbecue. I have choices at drive-throughs too. So why am I so disgruntled? Wouldn't you think I would be happy? Well, in truth, I should be. The problem is that we don't know how to be content—we just can't help ourselves. We look at people who have it better, got it easier, or enjoyed it earlier in life, and we are envious of whatever "it" is. Be it a vegan hot dog, a faithful partner, or a great job, we want to know where "ours" is when everyone else is devouring their abundant meals. Most of the time, it's right in front of us on our own plates! We have been blessed, but until we stop looking at everyone else's table, we will never know it.

Competition has its place. I work with larger companies than I used to, and I can understand how competition, when approached in healthy ways, can produce positive change. The flip side of competition is that it can also cause discontentment and yield needless frustration. Displaced comparisons can fuel jealously and insecurity—they rob us of the fruits of the Spirit. As Christians, we should strive to be content, trusting and rejoicing in all circumstances. As Paul shared with us:

> For I have learned in whatever situation I am
> to be content. I know how to be brought low,
> and I know how to abound. In any and every
> circumstance, I have learned the secret of facing
> plenty and hunger, abundance and need. I can
> do all things through Him who strengthens me.
> (Philippians 4:11–13 ESV)

Some circumstances are not fair, and they are not pleasant; some are downright painful. But when we count our own blessings and stop comparing our skills, homes, cars, jobs, families, and food to those of others, we will find that we have all we need— and probably even far more than we deserve. Trying to be the best, do the best, and have the best will exhaust you and rob you of your joy. Allow yourself to rest, because competition is exhausting. Learn to relax and let people eat their own dinner. Count your blessings, enjoy your food, and be grateful.

Chapter 24

✦◆✕◆✦

CROSSWALKS

There are little things that just annoy me. I am, after all, human. Though I am encouraged to walk in the Spirit, I still battle with the flesh. Today, the flesh got the better of me because something simple really burnt my biscuit! In case you were not raised in the South, if someone butters your biscuit, it means they did something nice and all is well. But to have your biscuit burnt means you are mad, as in "that really makes me want to throat-punch someone."

Let's first come to the agreement that crosswalks are in place for a reason: safety. I value safety, and so I use crosswalks. It annoys me when people don't. Today, I watched a young man walk just a few steps beyond the crosswalk and opt instead to cross a busy street literally just feet from the crosswalk. He walked right past the crosswalk to jeopardize his life. What was he thinking?

Probably the young man was thinking the same thing we are thinking when we deliberately neglect Biblical principles. Those consequences are not for me. It won't happen to me. How often do we walk right past the provisions of Christ and instead risk everything for a moment of ignorance and maybe excitement? I do it far more than I care to admit, and probably much like the young man, I've done it so often that I don't even consider what I am doing when I repeat my error. It is just what I have always done.

I truly doubt the young man walked past the crosswalk thinking, "Oh yeah, I'm a rebel. Watch as I defy the law and endanger my life." Yet that's what he did. That's what we do too. We've become comfortable in complacency and often lean heavily upon our own ideologies to the neglect of scripture. Without thought, we fail to apply biblical principles to our professional and personal lives. We are unintentional rebels—we are foolish.

It's not difficult to pick up our Bibles and read a few passages each day. It's easy, really. The problem is that it is also easy not to do so. It's not hard to walk a few feet to the crosswalk, but it's also easy not to do so. So we must make a decision. If we use the crosswalk, we are offered more safety. The odds are in our favor that we will cross the street without negative impact. By choosing not to use the crosswalk, we may make it across the street, but there is considerably more at stake. In the same way, when we adhere to biblical principles in our lives, crossing the street becomes less stressful because we are crossing in the security and provisions of Christ.

I may never be able to see someone ignore a crosswalk without experiencing distress. I'm serious—it really just irritates me so badly! But I will also be reminded that I have often ignored the safety of God's provisions and extend grace as grace has been extended to me. Having said that, if you catch yourself ignoring a crosswalk and look up and see a little red car literally explode with flames from the driver's seat, please know that it is a direct result of my blood pressure going through the roof. Be blessed and be safe.

Chapter 25

❖◆❖

OBEDIENCE

Rarely do I carry cash. It is just inconvenient. However, a few weeks before Christmas someone gifted me with a wonderful, crisp hundred-dollar bill. I was grateful. To say that I am frugal is an understatement. I grew up learning to save money. I don't need a lot of extras, and my biggest indulgences are books from Amazon and running shoes. I feel physically ill at the thought of wasting money or spending it recklessly. I wasn't raised to spend carelessly. So here I am with this wonderful cash in hand and thoughts of what to do with it!

I held on to it for two weeks with thoughts of a fancy dinner or maybe an extra pedicure—perhaps a few new books! My mind danced with possibilities. My mind was still doing an excited little jig as I walked into the salon to get some "woman things" tended to. You can imagine how my already prancing mind rejoiced to learn that the service rendered would be complimentary. No charge! Yay! But then it happened …

The young woman waxing my eyebrows began to talk about her four children. Her eyes absolutely became shining beacons of joy as she shared story after story. She blessed me so much with her enthusiasm for being a mom and a wife. She was attractive to begin with, but by the end of my few minutes with her she was gorgeous. Kind people will always be attractive. It was then that I felt I needed to give her my wonderful hundred-dollar bill. At first I said no to the prompting. In fact, I physically reached into my pocket just to ensure that magical forces had not removed it without my knowledge. It was there. I touched it again just to be sure. Seconds earlier I had been so excited and giving thanks for a free service, and there was no way I now was being asked to relinquish my prize! But that is exactly what I was being asked to do.

I truly believe I felt God urging me to bless this sweet woman. Now, I know that scripture tells us that God loves a cheerful giver (2 Corinthians 9:7). I pray that He also cherishes an unenthusiastic one. I handed the woman my $100 and said in a voice that belied my hesitancy, "I want to give you this. I want you to know how beautiful and rare you are, and I want you to know how much God loves you." The words were not my own. God was speaking through me with words of affirmation that this woman needed so badly to hear. Immediately, my reluctance turned to joy, and we celebrated together with tears, smiles, and hugs before I left the salon. What a blessing ... for me!

Good things happen when we act in obedience to God's promptings. Not only was I later surprised to receive more than triple that amount unexpectedly, but I felt such peace in my spirit. I felt honored that God had used me in such a way. I found myself reflecting on a time when I barely had money to pay my bills. I remember ordering off the dollar menu and then dividing the small meal in two so that I could also eat the next day. I believe with all my heart that when God blesses us, as He has me, we have a responsibility to bless others even when we don't feel like it—even when we have clung snugly to cash on hand for weeks!

Obedience isn't always what we would choose. It doesn't always feel good, and it certainly isn't always easy. Yet obedience to Christ is more precious than sacrifice (1 Samuel 15:22). If you have been blessed, bless others—and not just with cash. If you have been given a gift, use it to honor God and to serve others. Sometimes your time is what is needed. If God asks you to listen to someone, do it. It can be as simple as treating people respectfully and restoring dignity where it has been lost. Be kind, and be generous with your talents, your time, and your resources. Be obedient as good stewards of God's grace (1 Peter 4:10). Bless and be blessed.

Chapter 26

———◆►✕◄◆———

A GOOD REASON

Why am I late? Because my dog is ten years old. He's arthritic and has special needs ranging from asthma to hypoglycemia. He has good days, bad days, and in-between days. He rarely has great days when he feels like playing. So when he does have those unusual great days, I stop whatever I'm doing and play with him. And that is why I'm late. I probably should apologize, but I don't because I wouldn't mean it. I have made a choice for which I am simply not sorry. Those five to ten minutes I spent on the floor playing with my sweet, aging baby dog were the best minutes of my entire day.

Sometimes we are too hard on folks. We put our business britches on, and we assume that our work is the most important thing in the world to everyone. We forget that people have families, priorities, and problems that we know absolutely nothing about. We become trapped in a cycle of believing everyone sees everything from our perspective. We make the mistake of assuming that our focus is universal. When we experience anything that contradicts this belief in a single shared perspective, we become frustrated. After all, playing with your dog is a silly reason to be late for a meeting. But is that necessarily the case?

You see, I adopted my dog at a time when my heart was breaking. I won't go into details, but I can tell you that it was one of the darkest times of my adult life. I was overwhelmed with grief and exhaustion. Getting out of bed took courage that I just didn't have on most days. But then God gave me Oscar. I had to get out of bed to take him outside. I had to go to the store to get him food and supplies. Soon he was waking me up with snuggles and kisses, and I found myself able to smile and even laugh. My dog is and will always be one of my favorite blessings. To me, playing with him at inconvenient times is not silly at all. Indulging him is the least I can do.

I guess the point of this is that someone who is not normally late or someone who unintentionally smarts off in a discussion, or basically anyone who acts out of character, should occasionally be offered a bit of grace. Now, if someone is habitually late or routinely rude, that's a totally different situation and should be addressed appropriately. What I'm talking about is those people who have rare moments that don't make sense to us. We are all imperfect humans. For all the ways we are similar, there are a million ways in which our lives are different. Those differences should be respected.

Justice has its place, but so does grace. This week let's really try to be understanding and kind. Take a minute and breathe. Also, it doesn't hurt to remember that dog people are good people. Now if a cat person is late ... of course I'm kidding! Cat people are OK too!

Chapter 27

———◆◆◆◆———

BEING ENOUGH

I caved. I haven't worn eyeliner in years except when my team puts it on me before an event. I hate it. I don't like makeup, as I've probably made quite clear. But as I said, I caved. I searched YouTube for tutorials about applying eyeliner. I figured a quick three-minute video and I'd be an expert. After all, YouTube had taught me how to cut my hair and groom my dog during quarantine—sort of.

I searched for eyeliner for women in their fifties. Yes, I know that I am twenty years away from that mark, but I figure if I can just learn that technique now, it will spare me from having to watch this type of tutorial again when I'm older. Efficient.

I clicked on one video, and it became a three-step process with two different products. Too much. I exit the screen and click on another. This one showed a quick and easy way to apply eyeliner with only one product. I was sold until it said, "We have just demonstrated the wrong way to do this." The video then began to highlight all that was wrong with the results the simple technique had rendered. I am annoyed beyond words.

One final attempt, presented by an ophthalmologist, tells of the dangers of eyeliner. Yes, there are dangers! Like blocked glands, dry eyes, and infections. That is enough for me to decide to forgo my attempts to accept eyeliner.

Why do we do this to ourselves? What is the cost of beauty, and what do we really hope we will accomplish? Are social pressures so intense that we value appearance over health? Is it our own opinions we are trying to influence, or are we trying to convince others that we are acceptable?

When I was twenty-five, I got breast implants at the urging of my second husband. They were uncomfortable and made me more self-conscious than attractive. They ruined my runs. Breast augmentation is obviously not performance enhancing. I made the decision to have them removed without a corrective lift. Sure, my natural and now scarred breasts did not open as many doors in and out of bars or buy me any drinks, but it was time to stop drinking anyways. Not only did I feel better, but the doctor who removed the implants showed them to me, and one was leaking. I had kept all my follow-up appointments, and the original doctor who had placed the implants had not noticed or even suspected a leak. Dangerous. Not to mention that all of this was ridiculously expensive.

I will never judge anyone for having procedures or wearing eyeliner. I think if it makes you feel better about yourself and you can afford it, go for it. I just want us to be aware of *why* we're making the choices we do. If it is to earn someone else's approval or acceptance, my heart breaks for you. I've been there and done that, you will never be enough for some people. That's their problem, not yours.

Today, I am sitting and reflecting upon what I have gone through to be accepted. I think we all go through a lot to be recognized and approved of. I wish I had known in my twenties that God had designed me exactly as He wanted me to be. The point of this isn't to rant about the cosmetic industry or even to go on and on about the unfairness of social standards as it pertains to acceptance. The point is that if I had known twenty years ago what I know now, I would've relaxed a little. I definitely would have made my relationship to Christ more of a priority. I would have gone back to school sooner too.

If I could tell the younger version of myself one thing, it is this: "You are enough." No one ever told me that I would be fine on my own. No one ever told me that I didn't need to impress anyone. No one ever told me that it was OK to realize that I don't like to feel uncomfortable and can choose not to wear tight clothes or pantyhose! Oh, if I had known that I could be me, fearfully and wonderfully made (Psalm 139:14) just the way God intended me to be!

Now I am older. My body is healthy. Sure, there are parts of myself that I'm not overly pleased about, but overall I'm not too bad on the eyes, if I do say so myself. I read an excellent book about a woman overcoming an eating disorder. After years of standing in front of a full-length mirror and ritualistically condemning every flaw, she decided to do something different one day. At or near fifty years old, she challenged herself to look in the same mirror and say only nice things. She described it as feeling awkward and uncomfortable but liberating. She went from her head to her lower body, describing things that she was pleased with and surprised to find several.[2] Be brave and do the same thing! You will find that you are beautiful. And if you still want to wear the eyeliner, by all means wear it—but do it because *you* want to. And if you don't, don't. That's OK too.

Charm is deceitful, and beauty is vain,
but a woman who fears the LORD is to be praised.
Proverbs 31:30 ESV

---

[2] L. Kaeser, *Eating by Faith: A Walk with God. My Eating Disorder from the Inside Out* (Bloomington, IN: Balboa Press, 2016).

Chapter 28

---❖---

STRAIGHT AHEAD

I recall a time several years ago when I was running a half marathon. I've never been what would be considered fast. But that day, miracles aligned, and I set a personal record. I didn't stick around for the awards ceremony because it was cold and I was tired. I didn't figure I had even come close to placing anyway. A few days later, a friend of mine came across the results of the race, and guess what? I came in fourth in my division. That's one spot away from officially placing and taking home an award. My friend offered his condolences as he pointed out that I had "come so close." He asked if I was disappointed.

How could I have been disappointed? I knew I ran as hard and as fast for as long as I could. Had I started walking before I felt bolts of lightning shooting through both of my shins and fire in my lungs, then I would've been disappointed. I ran my best race, and I was thrilled. It's not a bad thing to come in fourth when you deserve to come in fourth. It's only disappointing when you know in your heart that you could've placed higher if you had only pushed just a little harder.

People leave a lot on the table because they start walking too soon. Things get a little uncomfortable, and that's enough to duck out of the race. Be it a rejection, a setback, a pandemic, or tired muscles and burning lungs, people find reasons to shut down and give up when the going gets tough. I've done it too. I bet we all have. Our partners come to us with confessions, and we opt for divorce instead of marital counseling. Someone less qualified is offered a promotion that we deserve, so we resort to looking for another job instead of accepting constructive criticism and growing where there is opportunity for personal development. Jumping ship is easier, right?

Even now as I sit and write this, I am drained. I couldn't sleep last night, and today left little to no time for a break. Several times, I was tempted and teased by the allure of canceling appointments, skipping runs, and rescheduling calls. I wanted so badly to slide paperwork off until the always elusive "tomorrow." I did none of these things. I made myself some green tea and went back to work. I set timers, because surely I can focus on the task at hand for ten minutes. Surely I can make just one more call.

There is something richly rewarding in having given your all to your work. There is something beautiful in exhaustion. It's not a healthy perpetual cycle to run yourself ragged, but there is something satisfying about knowing you didn't quit or give up. It feels much better the next day too—after your effort is rewarded by a great night's sleep and you wake up to a much lesser to-do list the next day.

We have all hit walls where it seems progress is impossible. Worse yet, we get comfortable with a level of success that demands nothing more of us. We stop pushing against the odds. We stop silencing the critics with our success. We stop giving of our energies, our talents, and our time prematurely, when there is still so much left on the table.

There is a time to slow down—when lightning is piercing through your shins. But don't stop pushing until then. Run your race, your career, and your life in a way that makes you proud. Regardless of where you end up, it will be much farther ahead than where you will be if you give up. Keep going. Keep pushing. Keep working. Keep reading the books that inspire you. Keep exercising. Keep eating right. Keep learning. Keep communicating with your family even when it's difficult. Keep forgiving. Keep listening. Keep praying. Keep running because only you can run your race, and it's up to you to place where you deserve—to live the life that your efforts earn.

Chapter 29

---◆◆×◆---

SALSA PANTS

It's no secret that I've put on a few pounds in the last year. I'm actually mostly OK with it. More to love, right? The only problem is I'm not comfortable in my clothes anymore. This is a bigger problem to me than it is for most because I have another problem: I hate to shop! The thought of trying on clothes and spending money on new duds just fills me with annoyance and dread. However, I recently went into a store and made a purchase that made me so happy that it inspired a second trip to the store and another purchase of the same jeans in a slightly different denim hue.

The design was brilliant! They were jeans but with a discreet little elastic band hidden in the waist. Brilliant! Never in all my life had I been so comfortable in a pair of jeans. I was thrilled. I told every female friend I knew that they "had" to go buy some of these jeans. I sent pictures to them so they would get the right brand and style. I wrote a review, for crying out loud! I became an unsolicited brand ambassador for these jeans.

Then something happened that humbled me to my core. Someone informed me that my favorite jeans were actually maternity pants! I was so embarrassed that I could have just died. But I didn't. Instead, I let the feeling of embarrassment wash over me quickly as I slid into my "maternity" jeans and set out for date night at La Hacienda. Tonight they were not maternity pants at all. They became chips, salsa, and queso jeans!

Just because someone somewhere at some point in time gave you a label does not mean that label has to define you. Sometimes we give ourselves labels and they stick. Our opinions of ourselves can be self-limiting and destructive. Maternity pants? That is someone's opinion. The greatest thing since sliced bread? That's mine. Too talkative? Someone else's. Fabulous company? Mine. Hyperactive? Theirs. Energetic and creative? Mine. We make a choice in what we believe about ourselves, but sometimes the world is so careless with labels that we get caught up in them and they overwhelm us.

My professor reminded me this morning of a quote from Viktor Frankl, a Nazi concentration camp survivor: "Everything can be taken from a man but one thing: the last of the human freedoms—to choose one's attitude in any given set of circumstances, to choose one's own way."[3] Frankl believed that life has meaning in any circumstance. I share this belief. I feel that meaning should not be defined by what situation we find ourselves in or the labels carelessly assigned to us, but in what we choose to learn from any given situation—the good we choose to see from day to day in others and in ourselves.

---

[3] Viktor E. Frankl, *Man's Search for Meaning* (Boston: Beacon Press, 1966), 104.

It is sometimes tricky to separate truth from fiction. The world hammers us with what we are and what we are not. Commercials tell us that we are too thick, our teeth are not white enough, and our clothes are out of style. We are desperate and lonely. Our situations are drear but not to fear—their products and services will solve all our problems! Thankfully, as children of God, we can choose to look beyond these lies and know with certainty what we really are: forgiven (1 John 1:9), loved (John 3:16), and chosen (Deuteronomy 14:2).

Your past, genetics, financial situation, relationships, and other external factors may tell you that you were designed to be in maternity pants. But I am here to tell you, my beautiful friend, that you were made for more. You, honey, were made for salsa!

Chapter 30

———◆✕◆———

FAITH AND RAIN

I roll my eyes and look out the window. The sun would be nice, but it's raining again instead. I wonder why I can't have snow and sunshine concurrently all the time. Of course, some people enjoy storms. The weather will never be ideal for everyone.

So because it can't be perfect outside, I surrender to the shelter inside my home. I try to find solace in knowing that somewhere someone is laughing with pleasure at being in the rain. Still, the thunder makes me reflective, and my thoughts are not easily distracted from the past. I pick up a book and immediately think of the person who recommended it. A quick message and I am reminded that people are kind, God is good, and I am safe.

It seems too often that we waste sunshine, fearing the next storm or thinking about the last. The promotion we got passed over on, the relationship that didn't work out, or the words that broke our hearts. We are prone to get caught up in things that have gone wrong, and we rob ourselves of the joy that is ours. We waste good weather.

More and more in my life, I am realizing the importance of community. It's not like me to reach out to other people. I lie to myself all the time when I convince myself that words don't hurt me and that my independence is a strength. I convince myself that I am confident with what I bring to the table, and I certainly won't starve by myself. But the truth is, last Saturday I needed help. The girl who inspires others found herself anxious and, if I'm honest, a bit scared. There was a time in my life when I would not have humbled myself enough to ask for help, but we all need help sometimes.

In business and in life, get a mentor and be a mentor. Get a friend and be a friend. Forgive each other and trust each other. Be someone who can be trusted. Life is not something we should try to do alone. With all that we can do for ourselves, we can't do it all. Strong people break, and everyone gets lonely. No one is exempt from bad weather.

It sometimes takes someone amazing reminding us that without the storms the day could never shine so bright. As Mark R. McMinn wrote in *Psychology, Theology, and Spirituality in Christian Counseling*, "I wonder if beauty is more striking in the midst of pain" (p. xv). Certainly, not all storms can be avoided, but what a beautiful opportunity to trust God through them.

Sometimes it's the people we never expect whom we feel compelled to reach out to without knowing why. And when we do, we find exactly what we didn't know we needed so badly. Sometimes the storms rattle us to our core. Trust that the sun is still there even when we can't see it. God is still working even when we can't feel it. Our security is not in what we can see or feel, but in what our spirits testify to in faith. Like a message from someone amazing on a rainy day, faith is just more profound when it contradicts circumstances.

Chapter 31

———————◆※◆———————

SUNDAY POTLUCK

I feel uncomfortable. My spirit is unsettled. I sit in the small congregation where I felt so comfortable last week and feel only condemnation today. My mind races. I was up all night struggling with memories from my past. Embarrassment grips me. Shame shakes me. I found myself nauseous as I searched for property three states away. *A fresh start. I need a fresh start.*

Now I find myself entrapped at a potluck where I don't belong. I read too much into everything today. The pastor failed to speak to me. Surely he has met someone who knows who I used to be. Like Chandler and Ross on the *Friends* episode when the "we were on a break" saga began, I was finding the connection.

Every fourth Sunday, someone comes forward to share their stories of addiction and crime, and that person is celebrated. I would expect the same acceptance for my own colorful history, but I feel less than approved of in this moment. The embarrassment I feel is weighing on me like the humidity I endured the week I spent in southern Alabama a few years ago.

I repeat to myself a line from *The Search for Significance*: "Confess your sins, worship God, and get on with your life."[4] I am trying but I am failing. It's not that I doubt my forgiveness. I feel secure in God's grace. It's just the fear of being "found out." I feel like a phony, and I just know that everyone sees through my carefully fashioned façade.

I think that's why I enjoy jail and prison ministry so much. I feel like I can tell the truth—all of it. I feel like I can tell "my girls" about my horrid past and how God has saved me. They tell me that they actually think more of me after sharing. I wonder at the irony in how I can be more comfortable in a jail with felons than in a house of worship with other Christians. I look around and can understand how other people feel the same way. I wonder if anyone else here feels like they don't belong. In this moment, I feel like it is probably just me.

I watch as other people fill their plates and go back for seconds. I push a few pieces of cornbread around my plate and sip my coffee in what I hope is polite participation. My mind is elsewhere. I just want to go home. I want to run away. I do eventually politely excuse myself and go home and sleep. When I am ready to wake up, I force myself back to sleep. The nightmares that usually cause me to avoid sleep are preferable to the reality that is suffocating me this afternoon. I am in a weird place. I don't feel like doing anything.

When I finally find solace in the ability to put my thoughts into words on paper, I find God tenderly waiting to receive me. I look at what is true instead of the speculations that my mind

---

[4] R. McGee, *The Search for Significance* (Nashville, TN: Thomas Nelson, 2003), 108.

has created and the devil has manipulated into a full-blown spiral. My issues today have more to do with my faith than anything. I have allowed my past to overshadow the fellowship that was available to me. I have allowed fear to steal the joy that is rightfully mine as a child of God. I have wasted an afternoon. Truth be told, I doubt anyone was thinking about me or my past. They were there for God and good food.

Then I consider this: what if they really were looking at me with condemnation? I can't change their attitudes. I can't change my past. I can continue to trust God with my future and be a light as I move forward. That would be hard to do if I ran away.

I am given a beautiful vision of myself as a child in the arms of my Abba Father. I am tired, but I resist the urge to take a nap. I struggle against His embrace until I am free only to throw a fit in the corner. When I have completely exhausted myself and tears mix with the sweat from my resistance, I climb back into His lap, and He lovingly wraps His arms around me and rocks me softly into His peace. He is not angry with me and He does not turn me away, even though moments earlier I had fought against Him. He just continues to hold me and rock me tenderly. I once again feel adored, protected, and peaceful.

I allow myself to feel the moment deeply. I allow myself to be loved by my Father God. Every ounce of struggle I felt earlier subsides in His embrace. I am grateful. And all joking aside, I cannot believe that I allowed the devil to steal my joy and rob me of the opportunity to enjoy Ms. Deloris's no-bake cookies at the potluck!

Chapter 32

---•◆◆•---

WEBSITE WOES

First, let me say that the tech genius who manages my website is wonderful. God puts people into our lives and our businesses for a reason! I would never in a million years attempt to do my own taxes. I have a wonderful and intelligent tax professional for that. So why on God's green earth did I think I could make changes to my own website without Andrew's assistance?

Let me start from the beginning.

I had a little extra time and thought, *I can do this*. And I did ... sort of. I made a few changes to the home page and "About Me" page that went effortlessly. I was feeling proud of myself and was glad that I did not have to bother Andrew. After all, he is a busy professional, a loving husband to his gorgeous wife, and a father of two beautiful children. I justified my attempt in that way.

However, what a mess I made when I attempted to edit the "Book Autumn" page of my website! Suddenly, there were subheadings that mysteriously showed up, topics I did not endorse, and literally foreign languages. I could have cried. OK, I did cry a little.

I quickly jumped on my phone and sent off an onslaught of urgent messages to Andrew, explaining in obsessive detail and with an overabundance of crying emojis just what I had done, ending as I had begun: "Help me!!!!!!!" Then, with an intense fear of being forever fired as a client, I waited not so patiently for him to resolve my issues and bill me accordingly.

From a spiritual perspective, this is what happens in life too. We take control instead of taking our issues to God. We have a little extra time and a pocket full of justifications. We do all right in the beginning, and the devil dances deceitfully in our minds, convincing us that we can handle anything with our own resources, maneuverings, and manipulations. We are confident as we move forward with a mysterious and somewhat unsettling ease … until something happens, be it as simple as a muddled website or as severe as a family tragedy. Suddenly, our situation is far worse than before, and we cry out "Help me!"

Sometimes, the things that happen to us because of our own misjudgments provide for wonderful opportunities for reconciliation with Christ. As scripture reminds us, "pride goes before destruction, and a haughty spirit before a fall" (Proverbs 16:18 ESV). These falls lead to humble places where God's grace can multiply in our lives.

Returning to a professional perspective, I want to encourage you to learn from these experiences. Do not be impatient. Do not get cocky. Let your team help you. Sit down for this next word of advice because it may come as a shock: we do not know everything! Hire experts. Do not do your own taxes if you are not qualified. Do not wax your own eyebrows if you are not experienced, and do not attempt to change your own website if you have no clue what you are doing. God truly does place people in our lives for a reason. Trust His plan.

Chapter 33

MY MOUNTAIN EXPERIENCE

Today I found myself desperately needing to withdraw from the crowds and chaos to be alone with God. I had an intense desire for intimacy with Christ that could be soothed only by retreating to a mountain near my home for reflection and prayer.

The mountain is a strenuous hike, and because of my struggles with anxiety, I doubted I could be obedient in climbing it to the peak. I reluctantly thought, *I'll just go a mile up the hike.*

However, at the mile marker an older gentleman was sitting on a bench. As I turned around, the kind stranger said, "You can't turn around now. You're almost there!" With his encouragement I continued to climb until I reached the peak.

With this experience still fresh in my mind, I found one quote from an assigned reading project that truly resonated with me at this moment:

> We encourage partly by demonstrating the courage of our own convictions. We model encouragement to others by living encouraging

lives. Our lives suggest to others whether or not we have any reasons for hope.[5]

In deeper consideration of the quote, I wondered whether the gentleman's encouragement would have been as inspiring if he had uttered the same words from the base of the mountain. The answer is no—his words carried impact because he uttered them while resting after he had ascended and was descending the highest part of the mountain. He had been there and knew it was worth the extra effort. His experience gave me a reason to hope.

Likewise, our lives as Christians should be lived in such a way that our words encourage others who look at us for reasons to believe. This is reinforced in "how we live speaks volumes about our reasons for hope amid a discouraging world."[6] Just like the climb to the summit, life is difficult, and for this reason it becomes increasingly important to "shine as lights … so that in the day of Christ I may be proud that I did not run in vain or labor in vain" (Philippians 2:15–16 ESV).

For communication to be effective, it must also be true. In a world where "lying is so commonplace that it seems to produce little or no physiological arousal,"[7] communication is rarely as successful as it should be. In his book *Peaks and Valleys*, the medical doctor Spencer Johnson illustrates how "fear blocks you, but the truth helps you to succeed." The author also illustrates a profound truth in that the pain within the process

---

[5] Q. J. Schultze and D. M. Badzinski, *An Essential Guide to Interpersonal Communication: Building Great Relationships with Faith, Skill, and Virtue in the Age of Social Media* (Grand Rapids, MI: Baker Academic, 2015), 80–81.
[6] Schultze and Badzinski, p. 81.
[7] Schultze and Badzinski, p. 62.

of climbing from a valley can make you aware of a truth that you must acknowledge to grow.[8]

I became aware of a truth as I was climbing the mountain this morning. It occurred to me that fear has caused me to miss out on a lot of things. It is true that things in my past justify my fear. However, this justification does not make my fears rational now. I realized today that I have not invested in overcoming fears that are not reasonable and no longer useful for protection. I now am aware that I must intentionally tackle the difficult issue of differentiating between fears that are reasonable and those that are not.

In returning to my mountain experience, I was exhilarated at the affirmation of my faith as I trusted God to continue to the peak. Each day I am thankful for opportunities to climb symbolical mountains in situations and with people I care about. Each day I am thankful to learn more about myself and others. To share my experience in a way that brings encouragement, let me say that I have seen the peak, and there is hope!

As I was returning down the mountain earlier today, I coincidentally began following a group who were playing gospel music as they hiked down the rough terrain. It was wonderful to be able to listen to worship music and praise God and thank Him for His goodness. I pray that my life will continually reflect the courage of my convictions as I seek to honor God and encourage others.

---

[8] Spencer Johnson, *Peaks and Valleys* (New York: Atria Books, 2009), 61, 69.

Chapter 34

———◆✦◆———

ALMOST

I've done a lot of frightening things with enthusiasm that quickly collided with reality and turned into fear. I'm recalling a time now. I felt confident standing in line to the water park ride. By "confident," I mean that I surrendered to the promptings of my beautiful stepson's pleas for me to go down one of the highest slides in the park.

Just as it was our turn to climb into our floats, the workers shut down the ride because there was a snake in the pool at the bottom. I relaxed. I felt sure that the ride would remain closed. It did not. It opened seconds later as the situation was dealt with. Now, not only was my fear of heights and my lack of confidence in my ability to swim making me nauseous, but my fear of snakes also slithered into my mind.

Nonetheless, I felt OK as I got into the floatation device. As the ride started, my enthusiasm turned to panic and burst forth in an onslaught of words not appropriate for the adolescent ears of my innocent child smiling and laughing next to me. But when it was over, I almost couldn't wait to do it again … *almost*.

That's what writing and publishing a book feels like. The idea is exciting, the ride is frightening, and eventually you learn something about yourself and are thankful for the experience. You almost can't wait to do it again ... *almost*.

I must confess, even as I submit this manuscript, I am hesitant. I find myself once again opening my heart to the world, and that is an exciting and scary thing. I remember when I held my first book, *Prospering*, in my hands: it was a proud moment that lasted exactly three hours before panic set in. What have I done? People will know my secrets; they will reject me as a writer and possibly even as a decent human! And yet I am doing it again because somewhere in my chaos God continues to give me adventures and words that inspire others to keep moving forward.

Sharing my story is a frightening honor. I am, at the end of it all, grateful. This is my ministry, and hopefully this book, like *Prospering*, will leave folks with smiles and the reassurance that "those of us just trying to keep it together" can prosper in wonderful ways too.

I felt a heaviness in this manuscript that I didn't feel in writing my first book. I'd like to chalk that up to maturity. In actuality, though, the last couple of years have been heavy. From pandemics to political upheaval, we've covered a lot of unfamiliar territory in a short span of time. I applaud those who made it look effortless. I, on the other hand, have been a hot mess. As always, God has sustained me and blessed me in spite of myself.

I pray that God blesses you as we continue this adventure of life. I don't know what will happen next, but I am grateful for every opportunity to find out. Climb the mountain, eat the donut, ride the ride. Most important, know that Jesus loves you. I pray that regardless of what comes next, you find yourself blessed with His peace. I pray that you laugh freely and rejoice always.

With all my heart,

Autumn Smith

Autumn Smith is available for speaking events. To book her to speak to your group, contact her through her website, www.autumnsmithinspires.com.

Printed in the United States
by Baker & Taylor Publisher Services

Printed in the United States
by Baker & Taylor Publisher Services